Famous Medieval People

by Grace Hansen

Abdo Kids Jumbo is an Imprint of Abdo Kids
abdobooks.com

abdobooks.com

Published by Abdo Kids, a division of ABDO, P.O. Box 398166, Minneapolis, Minnesota 55439.
Copyright © 2026 by Abdo Consulting Group, Inc. International copyrights reserved in all countries. No part of this book may be reproduced in any form without written permission from the publisher.
Abdo Kids Jumbo™ is a trademark and logo of Abdo Kids.

Printed in the United States of America, North Mankato, Minnesota.

052025

092025

Photo Credits: Alamy, Getty Images, Shutterstock

Production Contributors: Teddy Borth, Jennie Forsberg, Grace Hansen
Design Contributors: Candice Keimig, Pakou Moua

Library of Congress Control Number: 2024947601

Publisher's Cataloging-in-Publication Data

Names: Hansen, Grace, author.

Title: Famous Medieval people / by Grace Hansen

Description: Minneapolis, Minnesota : Abdo Kids, 2026 | Series: The Middle Ages | Includes online resources and index.

Identifiers: ISBN 9798384905288 (lib. bdg.) | ISBN 9798384905981 (ebook) | ISBN 9798384906339 (Read-to-me ebook)

Subjects: LCSH: Civilization, Medieval--Juvenile literature. | Social history--Juvenile literature. | Middle Ages--Juvenile literature. | Medieval history--Juvenile literature. | Dark Ages--Juvenile literature.

Classification: DDC 940.1--dc23

Table of Contents

The Middle Ages

The Middle Ages, or medieval period, was a time in European history. It lasted from about 500 to 1500 CE. Many important people lived during this time.

Europe
Asia
Africa
N
E
S
W

Famous Medieval People

Francis of Assisi lived from about 1181 to 1226. He was made a **saint** in 1228. Francis believed that animals and nature should be treated with respect.

Marco Polo was an Italian explorer. He spent many years traveling through Asia. During his travels, Polo learned about important **cultures**, **customs**, and inventions.

Europe
Asia
Africa
Marco Polo's
Travel Route

Dante Alighieri was an Italian poet and writer. He is best known for his epic poem *The Divine Comedy*. It is about a trip through the afterlife.

FORMILLI

Geoffrey Chaucer was born in England in the mid-1300s. He was a writer and a poet. Chaucer has been called "the father of English literature."

orks of
offrey

HEREBEGINNETH THE TALES OF CANTERBURY AND FIRST THE PROLOGUE THEREOF

WHAN THAT Aprille with his shoures soote
The droghte of March hath perced to the roote,
And bathed every veyne in swich licour,
Of which vertu engendred is the flour;
Whan Zephirus eek with his swete breeth
Inspired hath in every holt and heeth
The tendre croppes, and the yonge sonne
Hath in the Ram his halfe cours yronne,
And smale foweles maken melodye,
That slepen al the nyght with open eye,
So priketh hem nature in hir corages;
Thanne longen folk to goon on pilgrimages,
And palmeres for to seken straunge strondes,
To ferne halwes, kowthe in sondry londes;
And specially, from every shires ende
Of Engelond, to Caunterbury they wende,
The hooly blisful martir for to seke,
That hem hath holpen whan that they were seeke.

BIFIL that in that seson on a day,
In Southwerk at the Tabard as I lay,
Redy to wenden on my pilgrymage
To Caunterbury with ful devout corage,
At nyght were come into that hostelrye
Wel nyne and twenty in a compaignye,
Of sondry folk, by aventure yfalle
In felaweshipe, and pilgrimes were they alle,
That toward Caunterbury wolden ryde.

Chaucer's collection of stories, *The Canterbury Tales*, is his greatest work. It is about a group of travelers who pass the time with a story-telling contest. Some of the travelers include a knight, a **miller**, and a cook.

Joan of Arc was a French **heroine**. She was born in France to a **peasant** family in the early 1400s. At this time, France was fighting England in the Hundred Years' War.

Joan felt called to join the French army when she was just a teenager. She dressed like a boy to trick the military into letting her fight. She helped lead the French to victory in battle!

Beatriz Galindo was born in Spain in the mid-1400s. She was a writer and the teacher of Queen Isabella of Castile. Beatriz was one of the most educated women of her time.

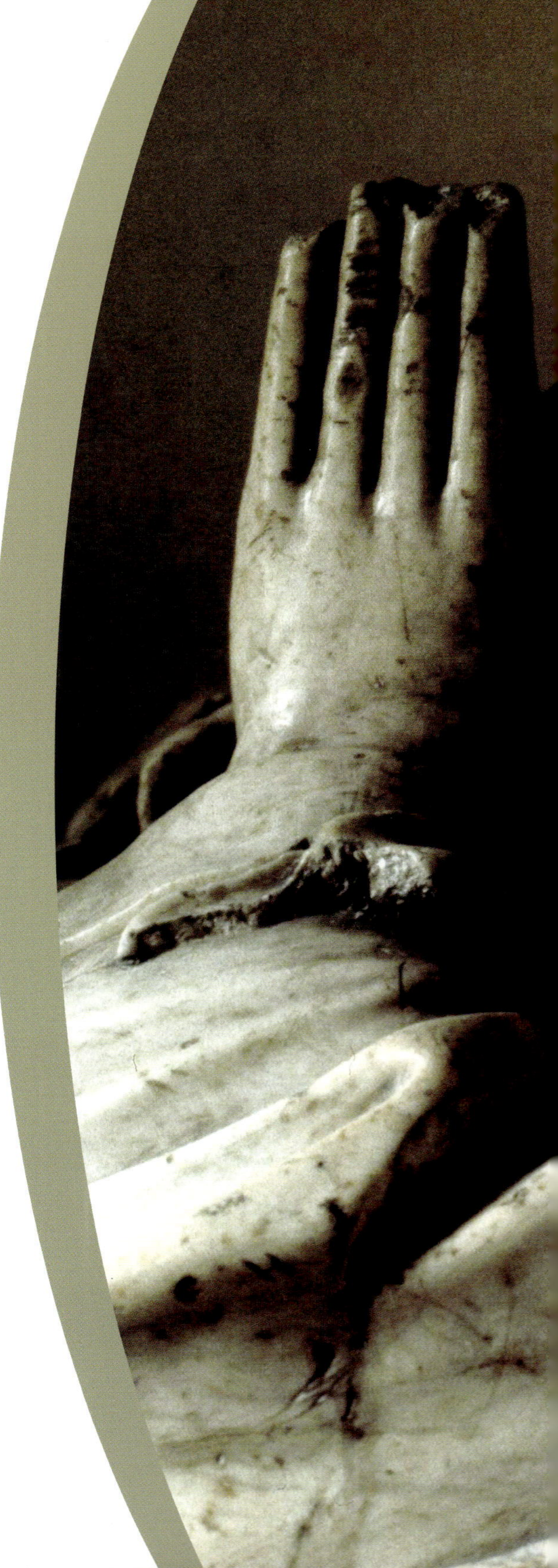

Timeline

Francis of Assisi

Dante Alighieri

Marco Polo

Geoffrey Chaucer

Joan of Arc

Beatriz Galindo

1100 CE | 1200 CE | 1300 CE | 1400 CE | 1500 CE

Francis of Assisi: 1181-1226
~45 years

Dante Alighieri: 1265-1321
~56 years

Marco Polo: 1254-1324
~70 years

Geoffrey Chaucer: 1343-1400
~57 years

Joan of Arc: 1412-1431
~19 years

Beatriz Galindo: 1465-1535
~70 years

Glossary

culture – the language, ideas, inventions, and art of a particular group of people.

custom – the usual way of doing things; the usual practice of a person or a group.

heroine – a woman who is looked up to for her courage, outstanding achievements, or noble qualities.

miller – a person who operates a mill. A mill is a machine that is used to grind grain.

peasant – a person who works on or owns a small piece of land. Many peasants were farmers.

saint – one who has been recognized by the Christian church as having lived a holy life.

Index

Visit abdokids.com to access crafts, games, videos, and more!

Use Abdo Kids code **TFK5288** or scan this QR code!